D1865220

A2 Listening

Ten practice tests for the **Cambridge A2 Key for Schools**

KET

A2

Anna Phillips and Terry Phillips

PROSPERITY EDUCATION

PROSPERITY EDUCATION

© Prosperity Education Ltd. 2025

Registered offices: Sherlock Close, Cambridge
CB3 0HP, United Kingdom

First published 2025

ISBN: 978-1-915654-51-9

Original edition © Innova Content Ltd.

This publication is in copyright. Subject to statutory exception and to the provisions of relevant collective licensing agreements, no reproduction of any part may take place without the written permission of Prosperity Education.

This edition is published by arrangement with Innova Content Ltd.

INNOVA CONTENT LIMITED
innova
INNOVATING LANGUAGE EDUCATION

The moral rights of the authors have been asserted.

'Cambridge A2 Key' and 'KET' are brands belonging to The Chancellor, Masters and Scholars of the University of Cambridge and are not associated with Prosperity Education or its products.

Designed by ORP Cambridge

Audio production by Wired Studios Ltd.

For further information and resources, visit:
www.prosperityeducation.net

To infinity and beyond.

Printed and bound by CPI Group (UK) Ltd, Croydon, CR0 4YY

FSC
www.fsc.org
MIX
Paper | Supporting responsible forestry
FSC® C013604

Contents

How to download the audio and transcripts

1. Go to www.prosperityeducation.net
2. Select the Downloads page
3. Select the book cover image
4. Enter password: **TIAB**
5. Download the audio .mp3 content
6. Download the transcript .pdf content

PROSPERITY ENGLISH

A digital platform for Cambridge exam preparation

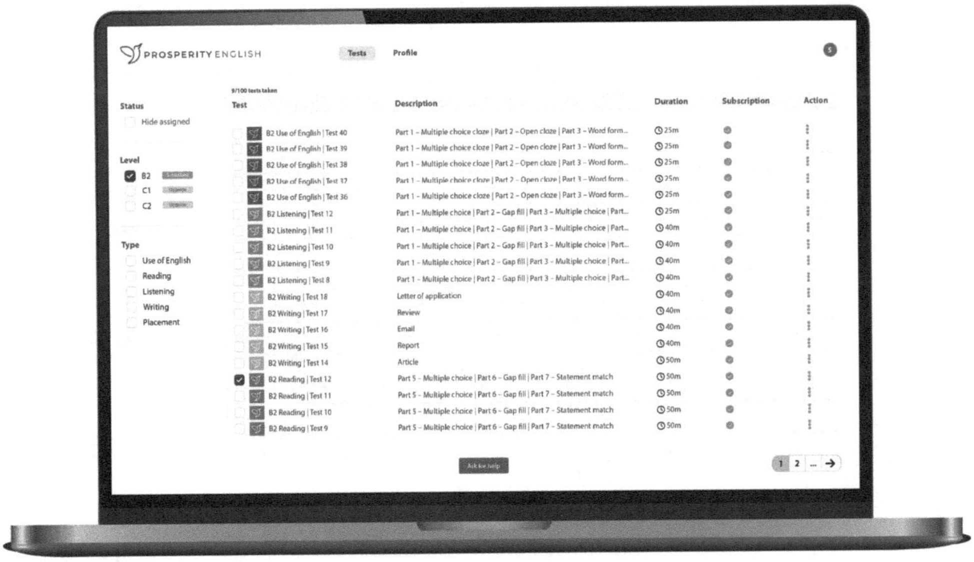

Prosperity English provides ample opportunities for repetitive practice, allowing you to reinforce your learning and improve your exam skills steadily.

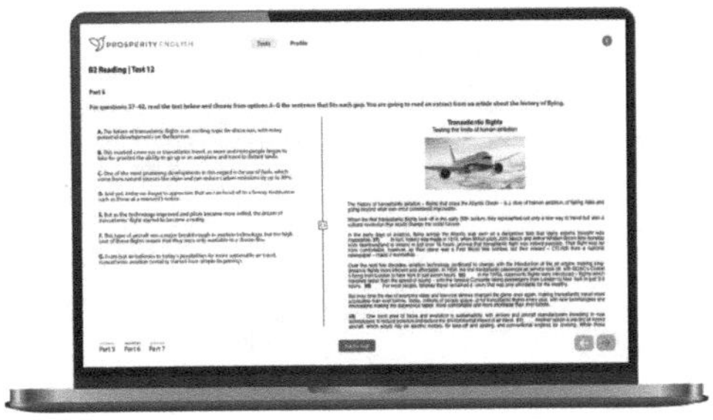

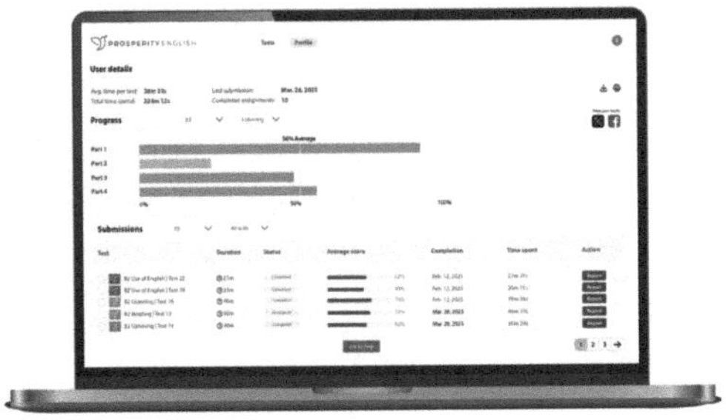

Try it for free

www.prosperityenglish.com

40% promotional discount code:
TIAB40

Introduction

Welcome to this edition of sample tests for the Cambridge A2 Key Listening, which has been written to replicate the Cambridge exam experience and has undergone rigorous expert and peer review.

The A2 Key English language exam is the second of six levels established in the Common European Framework of Reference (CEFR): A1–C2. Candidates of all ages can take the A2 Key test. In the exam you will have 30 minutes to complete the Listening paper. This section has five parts, and is worth 25% of the final score.

The tasks include:

- filling in missing words on a form while listening to one or two people speaking
- answering multiple-choice questions while listening to short and longer texts
- matching a list of nouns to people while listening.

You need to be able to:

- listen for important information in short and long conversations and monologues
- listen and write down important information and spell words correctly
- listen for the main idea or message in short monologues or conversations.

For more information, visit the Cambridge Assessment English website.

This book contains 10 Listening tests (Parts 1–5), comprising a total of 250 individual assessments. You or your students, if you are a teacher, will hopefully enjoy the wide range of texts and benefit from the repetitive practice, something that is key to preparing for this part of the A2 Key (KET) examination.

We hope that you will find this resource a useful study aid, and wish you all the best in preparing for the exam.

PROSPERITY EDUCATION
www.prosperityeducation.net

Cambridge A2 Key

Listening

Test 1

© 2025 Prosperity Education.
'Cambridge A2 Key' and 'KET' are brands belonging to The Chancellor, Masters and Scholars of the University of Cambridge and are not associated with Prosperity Education or its products.

Part 1

Questions 1 – 5

For each question, choose the correct picture.

---

1 Where did Mary go last Saturday?

A

B

C

2 How much are the train tickets?

A	B	C
£15.50	**£50.00**	**£15.15**

3 Who is Helen going to play tennis with?

A

B

C

4 What kind of film have they just seen?

A

B

C

5 How does George get to school each day?

A

B

C

Turn over ▶

Part 2

Questions 6 – 10

For each question, write the correct answer in the gap. Write **one word** or **a number** or **a date** or **a time**.

You will hear a teacher telling students about the school sports day.

School Sports Day

Day and date:	Friday 10th June
Place:	**(6)** Town ....
Starts:	**(7)** ....
Travel for students:	**(8)** school ....
Bring:	**(9)** ....
Go home from:	**(10)** ....

Part 3

Questions 11 – 15

For each question, choose the correct answer.

You will hear Katy talking to her friend Robert about her summer holiday.

11 Katy went away for

A nearly three weeks.

B three weeks.

C more than three weeks.

12 How long did the journey to the hotel take?

A three days

B six days

C two weeks

13 Where was the hotel?

A on the beach

B a ten-minute walk from the beach

C a ten-minute drive from the beach

14 Katy preferred

A not to go swimming.

B to swim in the sea.

C to swim in the hotel pool.

15 Katy spent most of the journey to and from Italy

A reading.

B playing computer games.

C looking at the countryside.

Turn over ▶

Part 4

Questions 16 – 20

For each question, choose the correct answer.

---

16 You will hear a teacher talking to her class.
What must each student do first?

A bring a letter from his or her parents

B pay for the trip

C give in a copy of his or her passport

17 You will hear a grandfather talking to his granddaughter, Betty, on the phone.
What's the weather like in Betty's town?

A It's snowing.

B It's raining.

C It's windy.

18 You will hear a teacher talking to one of his students called Lucy.
Why didn't Lucy do her homework?

A She forgot to make a note of the page numbers.

B She left her homework book at school.

C She was ill.

19 You will hear a boy, Oliver, talking about his hobby.
What has he just done?

A He has built a robot.

B He has won a competition.

C He has drawn a picture.

20 You will hear a man talking to his daughter, Julia.
What does he want her to do?

A her homework

B look after her sister

C the washing-up

Part 5

Questions 21 – 25

For each question, choose the correct answer.

You will hear Zoe talking to her teacher about a special day at school. What will each person help with?

Example:

O	Alice	B

Students

21	Daisy	☐
22	Kim	☐
23	Nick	☐
24	Ben	☐
25	Zoe	☐

Things to do

A	flags
B	food
C	drinks
D	timetable
E	music
F	balloons
G	quiz questions
H	tickets

Cambridge A2 Key

Listening

Test 2

© 2025 Prosperity Education.
'Cambridge A2 Key' and 'KET' are brands belonging to The Chancellor, Masters and Scholars of the University of Cambridge and are not associated with Prosperity Education or its products.

Part 1

Questions 1 – 5

For each question, choose the correct picture.

---

1 How did Katy get to school on Monday?

A

B

C

2 What time is the train?

A	B	C
4.30	4.45	4.15

3 What does William want for his birthday meal?

A

B

C

4 What is Holly's favourite subject at school?

A

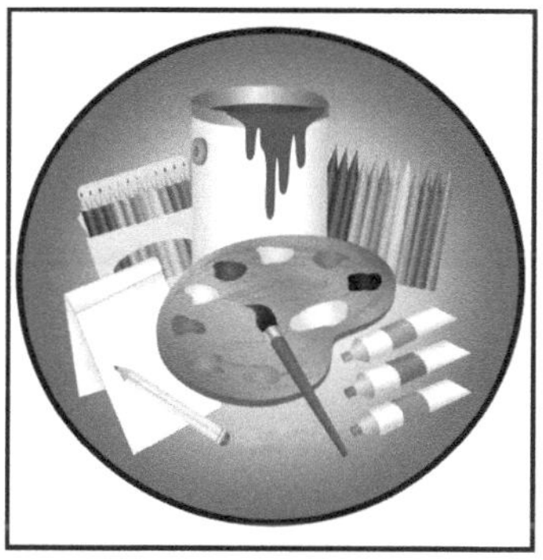

B

C

5 What is wrong with Harry's computer?

A

B

C

Turn over ▶

Part 2

Questions 6 – 10

For each question, write the correct answer in the gap. Write **one word** or **a number** or **a date** or **a time**.

You will hear a teacher telling students about a visit to a theme park.

Theme Park Visit

Day and date:	Monday ...21st October...
Place:	**(6)** .... World
Leave school at:	**(7)** ....
Price:	**(8)** ....
Teacher:	**(9)** Mr ....
Bring:	**(10)** ....

Part 3

Questions 11 – 15

For each question, choose the correct answer.

You will hear Emma talking to her friend Richard about her time off school.

11 How long was Emma in hospital for?

A three nights

B four nights

C five night

12 When did Emma start to feel ill?

A before dinner

B during dinner

C after dinner

13 She had

A a stomach ache.

B a stomach ache and a headache.

C a stomach ache, a headache and a temperature.

14 Why did the doctors make Emma stay in hospital?

A because they didn't know what was wrong with her

B because they knew what was wrong with her

C because they knew that she was frightened

15 Emma's parents didn't get ill because

A they didn't have the ice cream.

B they didn't have the rice.

C they didn't have the fish.

Turn over ▶

Part 4

Questions 16 – 20

For each question, choose the correct answer.

---

16 You will hear a headteacher talking to the whole school.
Where must students from E3 go this week?

A to the Science Lab

B to the East Building

C to W6

17 You will hear a father talking to his daughter, Helen.
What has she just done?

A She has fallen over.

B She has washed her hand.

C She has cut her hand.

18 You will hear a grandfather talking to his granddaughter, Alice, on the telephone.
What's the weather like in Alice's town?

A It's windy.

B It's sunny.

C It's raining.

19 You will hear a boy, Tom, talking to his parents about the summer holiday.
Where does he want to go?

A a park with space rides

B Spain or Greece

C a hotel with a swimming pool

20 You will hear a boy talking to his mother.
Why does he want to go to his friend's house?

A to play tennis

B to play some music

C to do Maths homework

Part 5

Questions 21 – 25

For each question, choose the correct answer.

You will hear Betty talking about birthday presents for her sister, May. What will each person give her?

Example:

O mother **B**

People			**Presents**	
21	father	☐	**A**	a snowboard
22	aunt	☐	**B**	a sweater
23	uncle	☐	**C**	shampoo
24	grandparents	☐	**D**	perfume
25	Betty	☐	**E**	gift card
			F	soap
			G	concert tickets
			H	a bracelet

PROSPERITY EDUCATION
www.prosperityeducation.net

Cambridge A2 Key

Listening

Test 3

© 2025 Prosperity Education.
'Cambridge A2 Key' and 'KET' are brands belonging to The Chancellor, Masters and Scholars of the University of Cambridge and are not associated with Prosperity Education or its products.

Part 1

Questions 1 – 5

For each question, choose the correct picture.

---

1 What language is Lily going to start learning next year?

A

B

C

2 What time does the film start?

7.15	**7.30**	**7.45**
A	**B**	**C**

3 Where did Mark meet his friends on Saturday?

A

B

C

4 Why is Anna feeling sad?

A

B

C

5 What is Matt going to play this afternoon?

A

B

C

Turn over ▶

Part 2

Questions 6 – 10

For each question, write the correct answer in the gap. Write **one word** or **a number** or **a date** or **a time**.

You will hear a teacher telling students about the school swimming competition.

Swimming Competition

Day and date:	Tuesday 21st May
Place:	**(6)** .... Pool
Starts:	**(7)** ....
Students from:	**(8)** Year ....
Number of events:	**(9)** ....
Bring:	**(10)** ....

Part 3

Questions 11 – 15

For each question, choose the correct answer.

You will hear Lucy talking to her friend Richard about her new house.

11 When did Lucy move house?

A at the weekend

B last month

C last Friday

12 Lucy's old house

A didn't have a back garden.

B didn't have a front garden.

C didn't have a garden.

13 Where is Lucy's new house?

A in West Road

B in Green Road

C in South Road

14 How does Lucy come to school now?

A She walks to school.

B She comes by car with her mother.

C She comes by car with her mother and her younger sister.

15 In Lucy's old house

A she had her own bedroom.

B she had to share with her younger sister.

C she had to share with her older sister.

Turn over ▶

Part 4

Questions 16 – 20

For each question, choose the correct answer.

---

16 You will hear a teacher talking to her class.
What must the students do at the weekend?

A go to the park or the river

B research the history of a local place

C choose a local building to research

17 You will hear a father talking to his daughter, Betty.
What will the weather be like on Sunday?

A There will be snow.

B It will be sunny and hot.

C It will be windy and cold.

18 You will hear a teacher talking to one of his students called Julia.
Why didn't Julia come to school yesterday?

A She had to go to hospital.

B She couldn't get a lift to school.

C Her mother was in hospital.

19 You will hear a boy, Michael, talking to his mother.
What has he just done?

A He has had an accident on his skateboard.

B He has broken a glass.

C He has dried the glasses.

20 You will hear a man talking to his daughter, Jane.
What does he want her to do?

A do the washing

B put the washing on the line

C take the dirty clothes to the kitchen

Part 5

Questions 21 – 25

For each question, choose the correct answer.

You will hear Sally talking with her mother about a special party. Each guest must dress up as a person with a particular job. What will each guest go as?

Example:

O Mary **F**

People			**Jobs**	
21	Clare	☐	**A**	a pilot
22	Robert	☐	**B**	an artist
23	Fred	☐	**C**	a musician
24	Sue	☐	**D**	a mechanic
25	Sally	☐	**E**	a farmer
			F	a doctor
			G	a photographer
			H	a police officer

Cambridge A2 Key

Listening

Test 4

© 2025 Prosperity Education.
'Cambridge A2 Key' and 'KET' are brands belonging to The Chancellor, Masters and Scholars of the University of Cambridge and are not associated with Prosperity Education or its products.

Part 1

Questions 1 – 5

For each question, choose the correct picture.

---

1 Which sport is Emma going to play at the sports centre?

A

B

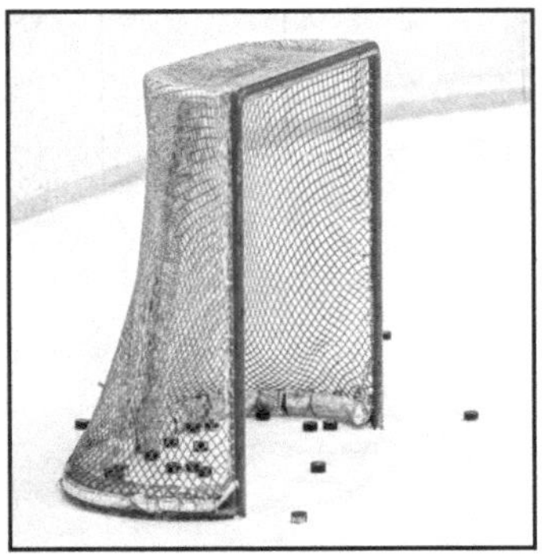

C

2 How much is the sweater which Katy likes?

£2.15

A

£25.00

B

£2.50

C

3 What is wrong with Jim's father?

A

B

C

4 Where is the teacher taking her class this afternoon?

A

B

C

5 Which room does Peter's mother want to change?

A

B

C

Turn over ▶

Part 2

Questions 6 – 10

For each question, write the correct answer in the gap. Write **one word** or **a number** or **a date** or **a time**.

You will hear a teacher telling students about the school fair.

School Fair

Day and date:	Saturday 11th November
Place:	**(6)** .... Hall
Starts:	**(7)** ....
Students to help from:	**(8)** Year ....
Price to parents:	**(9)** .... each
Brothers and sisters:	**(10)** ....

Part 3

Questions 11 – 15

For each question, choose the correct answer.

You will hear Charlie talking to his friend Julia about a television programme.

11 Why didn't Julia watch television last night?

A because she was typing up her school project

B because she was looking for pictures on the web

C because she was checking spelling and grammar

12 What did Charlie think of the programme?

A It was very good.

B It was quite good.

C It was really bad.

13 Charlie knew that

A Columbus thought the land was India.

B Columbus's sailor's wanted to turn round.

C Columbus went to America four times.

14 Why did Charlie watch the programme?

A because he likes historical programmes

B because there was nothing else on television

C because he found it by chance

15 Charlie

A is going to watch the programme this evening.

B is not interested in watching the programme.

C may watch the programme some time.

Turn over ▶

Part 4

Questions 16 – 20

For each question, choose the correct answer.

---

16 You will hear a teacher talking to one of her students called Jack.
How long will Jack be away from school for?

A six months

B a day

C two days

17 You will hear a man talking to his daughter, Vicky.
What does he want her to do?

A put the knives and forks on the table

B put the table in the kitchen

C put the plates on the table

18 You will hear a teacher talking to her class.
When must her students arrive at the school on Sports Day?

A one o'clock

B two o'clock

C two-thirty

19 You will hear a father talking to his daughter, Zoe.
What was the weather like on her camping trip?

A It rained a few times.

B It was sunny but cold.

C It was very hot.

20 You will hear a boy, Oliver, talking to his mother.
What has he just done?

A He has just packed his school bag.

B He has just brushed his teeth.

C He has just put his sandwiches in his bag.

Part 5

Questions 21 – 25

For each question, choose the correct answer.

You will hear Lily talking to her mother about the school photography competition. What photograph has each child entered for the competition?

Example:

O Mary **D**

People			**Photographs**	
21	Pat	☐	**A**	mountains
22	Dan	☐	**B**	a forest
23	Paul	☐	**C**	a beach
24	Mark	☐	**D**	an island
25	Lily	☐	**E**	a snow scene
			F	a field
			G	a desert
			H	a river

PROSPERITY EDUCATION
www.prosperityeducation.net

Cambridge A2 Key

Listening

Test 5

© 2025 Prosperity Education.
'Cambridge A2 Key' and 'KET' are brands belonging to The Chancellor, Masters and Scholars of the University of Cambridge and are not associated with Prosperity Education or its products.

Part 1

Questions 1 – 5

For each question, choose the correct picture.

---

1 What is Vicky taking to her grandmother in hospital?

A

B

C

2 Where did Peter stay during the summer holidays?

A

B

C

3 How much is the school trip?

£18.80	**£18.00**	**£80.00**
A	**B**	**C**

4 Why is Daisy feeling angry?

A

B

C

5 What time does the train get to North Town?

3.35

A

3.45

B

3.55

C

Turn over ▶

Part 2

Questions 6 – 10

For each question, write the correct answer in the gap. Write **one word** or **a number** or **a date** or **a time**.

You will hear a teacher telling students about a writing competition.

Writing Competition

Stories must be less than:	..........300..........	words
Send stories to:	**(6)** Mrs	
Competition closes on:	**(7)**	
Teachers will choose:	**(8)**	stories
Result before:	**(9)**	holiday
Winning prize:	**(10)**	gift card

Part 3

Questions 11 – 15

For each question, choose the correct answer.

You will hear Sarah talking to her friend Oliver about the school play.

11 When can people go and see the school play?

A all next week

B on Friday and Saturday next week

C on Saturday next week

12 Sarah's part in the play is

A more important than the king.

B in every scene in the play.

C the biggest part.

13 What does the king want?

A He wants his daughter to marry Fred.

B He wants his daughter to marry Hugo.

C He doesn't want his daughter to marry anyone.

14 Fred is really

A a rich prince.

B a gardener.

C a frog.

15 What does Sarah think?

A The play is good.

B Acting is fun.

C The queen is silly.

Turn over ▶

Part 4

Questions 16 – 20

For each question, choose the correct answer.

---

16 You will hear a teacher talking to her class.
What Maths homework must the students do this evening?

A Exercises 1, 2 and 5 on page 14 and page 15

B Exercises 1 to 5 on page 14 and Exercise 6 on page 15

C Exercises 1 to 5 on page 14 and page 15

17 You will hear a boy, Bill, talking to his mother.
What has he done this morning?

A He has made his bed.

B He has prepared some things in his bedroom.

C He has cleaned his bedroom.

18 You will hear a teacher talking to one of his students called Eva.
Why was she late this morning?

A The bus was late.

B The bus was early.

C She got to the bus stop late.

19 You will hear a father talking to his daughter, Mary.
What will the weather be like this afternoon

A There will be some rain.

B There won't be any rain.

C It will be sunny and hot.

20 You will hear a man talking to his daughter, Kim.
What does he want her to do?

A bring in the washing

B bring in the washing and put it in the bathroom

C put the washing in the bathroom

Part 5

Questions 21 – 25

For each question, choose the correct answer.

You will hear Daisy talking to her mother about her birthday party. What food will each person make?

Example:

O mother **B**

People

21 father ☐

22 uncle ☐

23 aunt ☐

24 grandma ☐

25 cousin ☐

Food

A roast chicken

B strawberry ice cream

C a salad

D burgers

E pasta

F pizza

G sandwiches

H sausages

Cambridge A2 Key

Listening

Test 6

© 2025 Prosperity Education.
'Cambridge A2 Key' and 'KET' are brands belonging to The Chancellor, Masters and Scholars of the University of Cambridge and are not associated with Prosperity Education or its products.

Part 1

Questions 1 – 5

For each question, choose the correct picture.

---

1 When is Richard going to go shopping with his mother?

A

B

C

2 Where will Peter meet Mary?

A

B

C

3 What time should Clare's father call back?

11.00

A

1.00

B

2.00

C

4 What was the weather like during Jane's holiday?

A

B

C

5 How much is the bracelet?

A	B	C
£20	£12	£15

Turn over

Part 2

Questions 6 – 10

For each question, write the correct answer in the gap. Write **one word** or **a number** or **a date** or **a time**.

You will hear a teacher talking to a group of students about the School Fair.

School Fair	
Day and date:	Saturday 3rd July
Tickets:	**(6)** .... for parents
Fair will be in:	**(7)** .... Hall
What to do:	**(8)** games, ... painting
What to buy:	**(9)** biscuits, drinks, ...
Time of fair:	**(10)** 2.00– ....

Part 3

Questions 11 – 15

For each question, choose the correct answer.

You will hear Matt talking to a school friend, Katy.

11 What was Katy doing when the accident happened?

A She was on her bike.

B She was in her mother's car.

C She was beside the road.

12 What did Katy do after the accident?

A She rode home.

B She couldn't ride her bike.

C She took a lift home.

13 In the accident, Katy

A didn't hurt herself.

B broke her thumb.

C broke her wrist.

14 Katy

A had an operation immediately.

B had an operation after two weeks.

C will have an operation in two weeks' time.

15 Why does Katy think she can do school work?

A because she can write with her right hand

B because she can move her fingers

C because she writes with her left hand

Turn over ▶

Part 4

Questions 16 – 20

For each question, choose the correct answer.

---

16 You will hear Eva talking to her friend Dan about something she has bought.
What has she bought?

A some clothes

B a model

C a board game

17 You will hear two friends talking about a painting.
What's the painting of?

A a garden

B a woman

C a house

18 You will hear Sarah talking to her father.
Why is she angry?

A Her friend took her History book.

B Her friend took her Science book.

C Her friend won't give back her Science book.

19 You will hear Molly talking to her friend Fred about her summer holidays.
Why does her family always go to Italy?

A Her mother buys clothes.

B They lie on the beach and swim in the sea.

C Her father likes sightseeing.

20 You will hear two friends talking about the next term at school.
What subject is the boy going to start?

A Spanish

B French

C German

Part 5

Questions 21 – 25

For each question, choose the correct answer.

You will hear Daisy talking to her friend about a school play. How will each person help?

Example:

O Daisy [F]

People			**Jobs**	
21	Nick	[ ]	**A**	lights
22	Alison	[ ]	**B**	tickets
23	Jim	[ ]	**C**	music
24	Kim	[ ]	**D**	drinks
25	Jack	[ ]	**E**	programmes
			F	clothes
			G	painting
			H	advertisements

PROSPERITY EDUCATION
www.prosperityeducation.net

Cambridge A2 Key

Listening

Test 7

© 2025 Prosperity Education.
'Cambridge A2 Key' and 'KET' are brands belonging to The Chancellor, Masters and Scholars of the University of Cambridge and are not associated with Prosperity Education or its products.

Part 1

Questions 1 – 5

For each question, choose the correct picture.

---

1 Where is Jill going with her parents at the weekend?

A

B

C

2 How much did May's mother pay for the sunglasses?

A	B	C
£15	**£50**	**£35**

3 What time does the film start?

A	B	C
2.15	**2.30**	**2.45**

4 How is Alice travelling to her grandparents' house?

A

B

C

5 When is Clare's birthday?

A

B

C

Turn over ▶

Part 2

Questions 6 – 10

For each question, write the correct answer in the gap. Write **one word** or **a number** or **a date** or **a time**.

You will hear a teacher talking to a group of students about a trip to London.

London Trip	
Day and date:	Friday 13th May
Cost:	**(6)** ....
Give money to:	**(7)** Miss ....
Leave at:	**(8)** ....
Bring:	**(9)** ....
Return at:	**(10)** ....

Part 3

Questions 11 – 15

For each question, choose the correct answer.

You will hear David talking to a friend, Vicky.

11 What is Vicky reading?

A a painting magazine

B a photography magazine

C a TV magazine

12 Vicky

A takes photographs with her phone.

B takes photographs with a camera.

C doesn't take photographs with a camera.

13 What does Vicky like painting?

A things from nature

B types of transport

C people

14 Vicky doesn't think she copies things because

A she takes lots of photos.

B she uses many photos to make one painting.

C she changes things in the photograph, like the light.

15 What does Vicky offer to show him?

A some of her paintings on her phone

B a photograph of one of her paintings

C one of her paintings

Turn over ▶

Part 4

Questions 16 – 20

For each question, choose the correct answer.

---

16 You will hear a girl talking to her friend about why she bought a hat.
Why did she buy it?

A for a wedding

B for work

C for her holiday

17 You will hear two friends talking about next term.
Which two languages is the boy going to choose between?

A French and Arabic

B Arabic and Chinese

C Arabic and French

18 You will hear a girl talking on the phone.
Why's she happy?

A The teacher let her enter the competition late.

B She has won first prize in the competition.

C She is in the last three in the competition.

19 You will hear two friends talking about a film.
What kind of film is it?

A a horror film

B a love story

C a comedy

20 You will hear Daisy talking to her friend, Harry, about her mother.
What's wrong with Daisy's mother?

A She has pain in her stomach.

B She has a temperature.

C She has problems with her heart.

Part 5

Questions 21 – 25

For each question, choose the correct answer.

You will hear Sue talking to her father about the timetable for her tests.
When does she have each test?

Example:

O Monday **F**

Days			**Tests**	
21	Tuesday	☐	**A**	Geography
22	Wednesday	☐	**B**	History
23	Thursday	☐	**C**	Chemistry
24	Friday morning	☐	**D**	English
25	Friday afternoon	☐	**E**	French
			F	Maths
			G	Physics
			H	Biology

PROSPERITY EDUCATION
www.prosperityeducation.net

Cambridge A2 Key

Listening

Test 8

© 2025 Prosperity Education.
'Cambridge A2 Key' and 'KET' are brands belonging to The Chancellor, Masters and Scholars of the University of Cambridge and are not associated with Prosperity Education or its products.

Part 1

Questions 1 – 5

For each question, choose the correct picture.

---

1 Where will Eva go at the weekend?

A

B

C

2 How much are the coach tickets?

A	B	C
£13.30	**£26.00**	**£13.00**

3 Who is Helen going to the basketball match with?

A

B

C

4 Where did the story of the film take place?

A

B

C

5 How is David going to his grandparents?

A

B

C

Turn over ▶

Part 2

Questions 6 – 10

For each question, write the correct answer in the gap. Write **one word** or **a number** or **a date** or **a time**.

You will hear a teacher telling students about a school trip.

School Trip

Day and date:	Wednesday 31st August
Place:	**(6)** .... Zoo
Leave at:	**(7)** ....
Travel:	**(8)** by ....
Price:	**(9)** ....
Bring:	**(10)** ....

Part 3

Questions 11 – 15

For each question, choose the correct answer.

You will hear Daisy talking to her friend Paul about her summer holiday.

11 How long did Daisy go away for?

A nearly two weeks

B two weeks

C more than two weeks

12 Why did Daisy and her family come back early?

A because the hotel was bad

B because the hotel food wasn't good

C because the restaurants were too expensive

13 Where was the hotel?

A on the beach

B a 10-minute drive from the beach

C a 10-minute walk from the beach

14 Daisy preferred

A not to go swimming.

B to swim in the sea.

C to swim in the hotel pool.

15 Daisy spent most of the journey to and from the hotel

A listening to music.

B playing computer games.

C looking at the countryside.

Turn over ▶

Part 4

Questions 16 – 20

For each question, choose the correct answer.

---

16 You will hear a teacher talking to her class.
What must each student do this evening?

A get his or her mother or father to sign the letter

B get his or her mother or father to send a letter about sports day

C get both parents to sign the letter

17 You will hear a father talking to his daughter, Julia, on the phone.
What's the weather like at Julia's summer camp?

A It's snowing.

B It's raining.

C It's sunny.

18 You will hear a teacher talking to one of his students called Molly.
What happened to Molly's homework?

A She forgot to do it.

B It's in the set of books.

C It fell on the floor.

19 You will hear a boy, Harry, talking about his hobby.
What has he just heard?

A A magazine is going to print his story.

B He has won a prize for one of his robots.

C He has received an email about his robots.

20 You will hear a man talking to his daughter, Sue.
What does he want her to do?

A write an email for him

B get the washing from the line

C put the garden chairs away

Part 5

Questions 21 – 25

For each question, choose the correct answer.

You will hear Alice talking to her teacher about the class party.
What will each person help with?

Example:

O Sam [A]

People			**Jobs**	
21	Hugo	☐	**A**	food
22	Holly	☐	**B**	balloons
23	Ben	☐	**C**	music
24	Charlie	☐	**D**	games
25	Alice	☐	**E**	drinks
			F	flags
			G	quiz questions
			H	hats

PROSPERITY EDUCATION
www.prosperityeducation.net

Cambridge A2 Key

Listening

Test 9

© 2025 Prosperity Education.
'Cambridge A2 Key' and 'KET' are brands belonging to The Chancellor, Masters and Scholars of the University of Cambridge and are not associated with Prosperity Education or its products.

Part 1

Questions 1 – 5

For each question, choose the correct picture.

---

1 Which subject is Vicky going to stop learning next year?

A

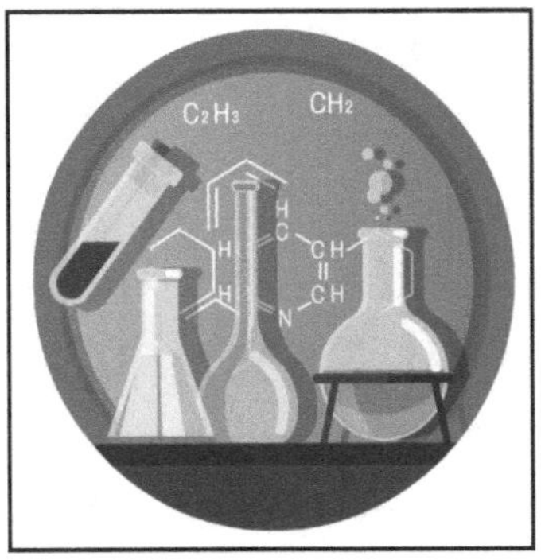

B

C

2 When does the volleyball match start?

3.00	**3.30**	**4.00**
A	**B**	**C**

3 Where did Hugo go at the weekend?

A

B

C

4 Why is Lucy feeling happy?

A

B

C

5 What has Fred just done?

A

B

C

Turn over ▶

Part 2

Questions 6 – 10

For each question, write the correct answer in the gap. Write **one word** or **a number** or **a date** or **a time**.

You will hear a teacher telling students about a school trip to a funfair.

Funfair Trip

Day and date:	Saturday ......15th July......
Place:	**(6)** .... Fair
Buses leave at:	**(7)** ....
Students from:	**(8)** Year ....
Number of rides:	**(9)** ....
Price:	**(10)** ....

Part 3

Questions 11 – 15

For each question, choose the correct answer.

You will hear Kim talking to her friend Ben about her new school.

11 How long has Kim been at the new school?

A a week

B two weeks

C a month

12 Kim thinks her new school is better because

A there are more sports fields.

B the teachers are better.

C the classrooms are better.

13 Where is Kim's new school?

A North Road

B White Road

C East Road

14 How does Kim go to school now?

A She walks to school.

B She goes in her mother's car.

C She goes by bus.

15 Kim's football team

A is playing against Ben's football team.

B is playing at Ben's school.

C is playing against a team from Ben's school.

Turn over ▶

Part 4

Questions 16 – 20

For each question, choose the correct answer.

---

16 You will hear a teacher talking to her class.
What must the students do this evening?

A choose a local place

B find out the history of a local place

C draw a map of the changes to a local place

17 You will hear a father talking to his daughter, Lily.
What will the weather be like on Saturday?

A It will be sunny.

B It will be warm.

C It will be cold.

18 You will hear a teacher talking to one of his students called May.
Why didn't May do her homework yesterday?

A She left her homework book at school.

B She couldn't understand the questions.

C She didn't know which page to do.

19 You will hear a boy, Jack, talking to his mother.
Why is he late?

A He had an accident.

B His friend had an accident.

C He has been to the hospital.

20 You will hear a man talking to his daughter, Jane.
What does he want her to do?

A finish her homework

B send an email for him

C help him wrap a present

Part 5

Questions 21 – 25

For each question, choose the correct answer.

You will hear Anna talking to her teacher about a school concert. What will each student do for the concert.

Example:

O Sue **F**

People			Instruments and things to do	
21	Jill	☐	**A**	guitar
22	Eva	☐	**B**	piano
23	Dan	☐	**C**	drums
24	Emma	☐	**D**	violin
25	Anna	☐	**E**	singing
			F	lights
			G	photographs
			H	adverts

Cambridge A2 Key

Listening

Test 10

© 2025 Prosperity Education.
'Cambridge A2 Key' and 'KET' are brands belonging to The Chancellor, Masters and Scholars of the University of Cambridge and are not associated with Prosperity Education or its products.

Part 1

Questions 1 – 5

For each question, choose the correct picture.

---

1 What is Sarah going to buy for her mother's birthday?

A

B

C

2 Where did Harry stay during the summer holidays?

A

B

C

3 How much are the plane tickets?

£90.19	**£19.90**	**£90.00**
A	**B**	**C**

4 What is Holly waiting for?

A

B

C

5 What time does the film start?

A	B	C
3.15	**3.45**	**2.45**

Turn over ▶

Part 2

Questions 6 – 10

For each question, write the correct answer in the gap. Write **one word** or **a number** or **a date** or **a time**.

You will hear a teacher telling students about a school trip.

The Water Park

Day and date:	Saturday 21st June
Cost:	**(6)** ....
Give money to:	**(7)** Mr ....
Leave at:	**(8)** ....
Return at:	**(9)** ....
Bring:	**(10)** ....

Part 3

Questions 11 – 15

For each question, choose the correct answer.

You will hear Kim talking to her friend Ben about a film which they have seen.

11 Why didn't Kim want to go to the film?

A because Ben said it was about people from other planets

B because it was about people from other planets

C because she thought it was about people from other planets

12 In the film, the other astronauts took off without the woman because

A they thought she was dead.

B they had to follow the timetable.

C she had an accident in her car.

13 What didn't Ben understand?

A who started the farm

B how the woman astronaut grew things

C why the woman astronaut needed to grow things

14 Ben thinks the end of the film is silly because they couldn't

A turn the spaceship round.

B know that she was not dead.

C fly back to the planet.

15 What did Kim think the film was about?

A finding answers to problems

B an astronaut living on a planet

C space and spaceships

Turn over ▶

Part 4

Questions 16 – 20

For each question, choose the correct answer.

---

16 You will hear a teacher talking to her class.
What History homework must the students do this evening?

A Exercises 1 and 5 on page 80

B Exercises 1, 4 and 5 on page 80

C Exercises 1, 2, 3 and 4 on page 80

17 You will hear a boy, William, talking to his mother.
What has he done this morning?

A He has cleaned his teeth.

B He has put his books in his school bag.

C He has had breakfast.

18 You will hear a teacher talking to one of his students called Grace.
Why wasn't she at school yesterday?

A Her train had an accident at Barton.

B Her train didn't go all the way.

C Her train didn't come yesterday.

19 You will hear a father talking to his daughter, Anna.
What will the weather be like tomorrow?

A There will be some rain.

B There won't be any rain.

C It will be sunny and hot.

20 You will hear a mother talking to her son, George.
What does she want him to do?

A the knives and forks

B the plates

C the glasses

Part 5

Questions 21 – 25

For each question, choose the correct answer.

You will hear Jill talking to her mother about her brother's birthday. What present will each person give him?

Example:

O mother **H**

People			Presents	
21	grandma	☐	**A**	a robot
22	father	☐	**B**	a car
23	uncle	☐	**C**	a plane
24	aunt	☐	**D**	money
25	cousin	☐	**E**	a book
			F	socks
			G	a shirt
			H	shoes

Answers

Practice Test 1 Listening

Part 1	5 marks
1	A
2	A
3	C
4	C
5	A

Part 2	5 marks
6	Stadium
7	10.30
8	buses
9	lunch
10	school

Part 3	5 marks
11	A
12	A
13	B
14	C
15	A

Part 4	5 marks
16	A
17	B
18	C
19	B
20	B

Part 5	5 marks
21	C
22	A
23	E
24	G
25	F

Practice Test 2 Listening

Part 1 **5 marks**

1	C
2	B
3	C
4	B
5	B

Part 2 **5 marks**

6	History
7	8.00
8	£15
9	Mr Brown
10	water

Part 3 **5 marks**

11	A
12	B
13	B
14	A
15	C

Part 4 **5 marks**

16	C
17	B
18	A
19	A
20	C

Part 5 **5 marks**

21	E
22	D
23	H
24	A
25	F

Practice Test 3 Listening

Part 1 — 5 marks

1	C
2	C
3	A
4	C
5	A

Part 2 — 5 marks

6	North
7	2.30
8	5
9	15
10	towel

Part 3 — 5 marks

11	C
12	A
13	C
14	C
15	B

Part 4 — 5 marks

16	B
17	C
18	B
19	B
20	C

Part 5 — 5 marks

21	C
22	B
23	G
24	D
25	A

Practice Test 4 Listening

Part 1 — 5 marks

1	C
2	B
3	C
4	B
5	C

Part 2 — 5 marks

6	Main
7	12.30
8	6
9	£3
10	free

Part 3 — 5 marks

11	B
12	A
13	A
14	C
15	C

Part 4 — 5 marks

16	C
17	A
18	B
19	C
20	B

Part 5 — 5 marks

21	B
22	F
23	A
24	G
25	H

Practice Test 5 Listening

Part 1 **5 marks**

1 C
2 B
3 A
4 C
5 C

Part 2 **5 marks**

6 Barnes
7 14th April
8 3
9 half-term
10 £50

Part 3 **5 marks**

11 C
12 B
13 B
14 A
15 B

Part 4 **5 marks**

16 C
17 B
18 C
19 A
20 A

Part 5 **5 marks**

21 D
22 C
23 G
24 E
25 F

Practice Test 6 Listening

Part 1 — 5 marks

1 B
2 C
3 B
4 A
5 A

Part 2 — 5 marks

6 £2.50
7 North
8 face
9 cakes
10 5.00

Part 3 — 5 marks

11 A
12 A
13 C
14 B
15 C

Part 4 — 5 marks

16 A
17 B
18 A
19 A
20 B

Part 5 — 5 marks

21 C
22 A
23 G
24 E
25 D

Practice Test 7 Listening

Part 1 — 5 marks

1 B
2 C
3 C
4 A
5 A

Part 2 — 5 marks

6 £35
7 Ball
8 8.30
9 water
10 5.00

Part 3 — 5 marks

11 A
12 B
13 A
14 B
15 B

Part 4 — 5 marks

16 A
17 B
18 C
19 C
20 A

Part 5 — 5 marks

21 E
22 B
23 A
24 C
25 G

Practice Test 8 Listening

Part 1 **5 marks**

1	C
2	A
3	C
4	B
5	B

Part 2 **5 marks**

6	Newton
7	8.30
8	bus
9	£10
10	umbrella

Part 3 **5 marks**

11	A
12	C
13	B
14	C
15	B

Part 4 **5 marks**

16	A
17	B
18	C
19	A
20	B

Part 5 **5 marks**

21	E
22	F
23	C
24	G
25	H

Practice Test 9 Listening

Part 1 5 marks

1 A
2 C
3 A
4 C
5 B

Part 2 5 marks

6 Bert's
7 1.30
8 4
9 12
10 £15

Part 3 5 marks

11 A
12 A
13 C
14 A
15 C

Part 4 5 marks

16 A
17 C
18 B
19 B
20 C

Part 5 5 marks

21 A
22 C
23 B
24 E
25 H

Practice Test 10 Listening

Part 1 5 marks

1 A
2 C
3 C
4 A
5 B

Part 2 5 marks

6 £15
7 Bell
8 8.30
9 4.30
10 lunch

Part 3 5 marks

11 A
12 B
13 B
14 C
15 A

Part 4 5 marks

16 C
17 C
18 B
19 A
20 A

Part 5 5 marks

21 F
22 C
23 B
24 D
25 E